Copyright © 2018 Kimberly Fitten

All rights reserved.

ISBN: 1-7324924-1-7

ISBN-13: 978-1-7324924-1-7

Greetings!

I am overjoyed that you are, at this moment, holding this journal in your hands. This is more than a journal, it is both a weapon and toolkit necessary for mentally securing the life you want and becoming the best version of yourself!

In Faith & Fabulousness,

Kimberly Fitten

Make Your Decree

My Story

Four years ago I was in a horrible place in every area of my life. Financially, I was making great money, but I was working harder and not smarter. I had three extra coaching contracts on top of my teacher pay, but that meant I had no free evenings, mornings, or weekends. I was a workaholic! I was exhausted and drained mentally, which was CLEARLY connected to the way I was filling my time. There was always a competition, practice, or grading to tend to and this cyclical black hole was nothing to look forward to. Physically, I was eating like it was going out of style. The guilt fueled my eating dysfunction, and I would starve myself or simply be too busy to bother with the business of sustenance. Spiritually, I was pissed because my prayers for marriage and motherhood had gone unanswered. I felt my years spent in a committed relationship was an incredible waste of life. I'd been overlooked for several promotions, and felt forgotten. I was 35, single, career-stagnant, and in a dead-end cul-du-sec of complaining. My awakening occurred at the hand of a candid friend who told me I needed to get my crap together. I went home and screamed at the top of my lungs "WHAT AM I MISSING? THERE'S GOT TO BE MORE!!!" I found myself on YouTube searching for anything positive.

Job 22:28

I searched for videos on "how to be positive" and that moment, that choice changed my life for the better. Literally, the next day I entered the workplace skipping and smiling. Nothing in my life had changed BUT my mindset. My outlook was different. I no longer felt I was a powerless passenger at the mercy of life. A few months after my shift in mindset I was promoted and found the time to start my own mentoring organization. Two years later I secured another position, wrote my first book, stepped up and out in ministry, and resigned from my coaching obligations. I started living my life in-purpose.

Make Your Decree

thou shalt also **DECREE** a thing. and it shall be **ESTABLISHED,** Unto thee.

Job 22:28

Congratulations!

What a Power Move! You made the choice to DECREE the life you always dreamed! This Journal is the 1st step to taking back control and seeing visible growth. In order to take full advantage of all of the tools this journal provides you will need to...

- *Have a clear picture of what your *best* self looks like.*
- *Be open to parting with restrictive thinking (tradition, negative self-talk, toxic environments)
- *Carve out "me" time.
- *Discipline yourself to be consistently committed to YOU!

Make Your Decree

Your thoughts shape Your words And your words shape, your world.

Job 22:28

When I first began to decree I saw results immediately because I was intrinsically motivated by my beliefs. Because I grew up watching my mother speak things into existence, believing in what I could not see came naturally. I did not realize that this wasn't the case for everyone. When I first started Morning Mindset (my Facebook Live) I was baffled by the amount of people who struggled to see the manifestation of what they decreed. The problem was that their beliefs did not match what they were speaking. It is more than words of hope, decreeing, is a way of life. Your mindset is the key to manifesting what you speak into the universe. The brain is the strongest most powerful muscle in the body, and if you can master your thought patterns you will MANIFEST!

How do you begin to master your thoughts?

1. Give yourself permission to see things in a different light.

2. Believe that it is your destiny to live the BEST life possible.

3. Remove naysayers and sources of negativity from your life.

4. See Everything working to produce your highest GOOD

What Does the Bible Say About It?

It is not uncommon for Christians to feel uncomfortable when they first begin affirming. They are conflicted because of one letter-- "I". One of my coaching clients told me "I just feel that using all of the 'I am' stuff eliminates my need for God, and I don't want Him to think I feel I can do it on my own…" **RELAAAAXXXXX**. The God made Universe is set up to respond to your Decree.

Job 22:28

Don't believe me? Check out the following:

- Prov. 15:4 Positive words bring life
- Prov. 18:4 Our words are a source of life-giving water
- Prov. 18:21 Life and death rest in our words
- Matt. 21:21 Have true faith in what you speak and you can move mountains.
- Mark 11:23 Speak without doubt and whatever you say will be done. Even to the extent of casting a mountain into the sea.
- Rom. 8:28 Heirs of God, since we are His children we have whatever HE has.
- Gal. 3:26 We are children of the God who spoke all things in existence.
- John 14:12 Since we are His children and believe, we have the power to do even greater works than our Father.
- **<u>Job 22:28 WE HAVE THE POWER TO DECREE AND WATCH IT HAPPEN!</u>**

Decree 101

You cannot **DECREE** if you do not know **WHAT YOU WANT**. Many of us make a common mistake by waiting until moments of contrast occur to begin affirming. Situational declarations **NEVER** manifest! In order to be effective you must believe and declare your destination.

The God made Universe does not understand sarcasm!

Only speak what you want to see because even your No is still a YES!

Ex: "I don't want to be poor" establishes that poverty is already a part of your existence. Instead Decree, "I am abundance and have all that I need!" If you are having trouble believing, DECREE the possibility!

Job 22:28

"I believe it is possible for me to live in abundance". All it takes is believing in the possibility to begin to change the trajectory of your thoughts.

How to Know What to Want?

Visualization is a key component to decreeing what you want, but quieting the mind can be difficult. It is imperative that you dedicate a minimum of 30 minutes to thinking about yourself. This time should be spent in your favorite place and with ZERO distractions so give yourself permission to UNPLUG for a bit. I promise you whatever it is CAN WAIT and YOU DESERVE "me" time.

My visualization space is a place of peace, warmth, nostalgia, and aesthetically pleasing. I sit on a plush fuzzy blanket, surround myself with pillows, play ocean sounds and set a small fan to low cool so I can feel a slight comforting breeze. I also burn sage and lavender oil and light a few candles to seal the feeling of a safe, comfortable space. Feel free to take a day to set up your space and then come back to this.

Let's Visualize!

The key to visualization is IMAGINATION! As children we used this without hesitation, but as we grew older we were told that playing "make believe" was childish and maturity was necessary. I'm sorry they lied to you, NEVER lose your IMAGINATION. IT IS A GIFT and you will use this gift every day for 17 seconds and for 30 minutes (I'll explain in a bit).

Job 22:28

Step 1: Think of what a limitless life would look like. Close your eyes and visualize the typical day of a limitless life.

Ex: I wake up and sit on my terrace with a cup of piping hot coffee. I have a beautiful garden filled with tiger lilies and lilacs that I gaze at while the sun beams upon my face. I am silent in a moment of thankfulness. I enter my bedroom and begin to get ready for my day. I am going to Atlanta for a women's conference, but I have a few meetings with influencers on potential collaborative projects so I have to be on my game. When my Uber driver arrives I leave in an all white pantsuit, the hair framing my face pushes away in the breeze as the rest cascades down my back. My assistant calls to give me the day's itinerary, and once again I'm off to connect people with their purpose and unlock their talents.

Step 2: Note what emotions were present in your typical day.

Ex: I felt the peace of the morning, excitement of meeting new people, joy of helping others, and thankfulness of a blessed life.

Step 3: Be still. Simply sit in the silence of the moment without writing, talking, or moving on in thought.

Ex: I sit quietly in the silence and become aware of the goodness around me. I then add the fuel of the Thankfulness

Step 5: Write down any new ideas, desires, emotions, inspirations, or answers revealed in your time of self-care.

Job 22:28

what we visualize **comes from** our desires, and what we **Visualize,** inspires what we decree.

Take a moment and record what you visualized. RECORD EVERY DETAIL- what you looked like, ate, where you lived, what you wore, spouse, children...etc. LEAVE NOTHING OUT!

My Visualization
_____
_____
_____
_____
_____
_____
_____
_____
_____
_____
_____
_____
_____
_____
_____
_____
_____
_____
_____
_____
_____
_____
_____

Job 22:28

Take a moment and list your desires. Remember to categorize them in order create an accurate picture of the life you want and leave nothing out.

My Desires

Financially

_____
_____
_____
_____

Physically

_____
_____
_____
_____
_____

Mentally

_____
_____
_____
_____

Make Your Decree

Relationships
_____
_____
_____
_____
_____

Career
_____
_____
_____
_____
_____

Purpose
_____
_____
_____
_____
_____
_____
_____

Job 22:28

"Whoever wants to embrace life and
See the day fill up with good,
Here's what you do:
Say nothing evil or hurtful"
1 Peter 3:10

Make Your Decree

Emotion is what fuels our tenacity and motivates us from within. Record what it felt like to visualize your limitless life.

Emotions
_____
_____
_____
_____
_____
_____
_____
_____
_____

Using your list of desires, and emotions generate declarations for every area represented in your moment of visualization. What you decree can start with "I AM" or it can be a simple statement of fact.

Ex: "I Decree I am successful in business." OR "I Decree The abundance of the universe flows to me and instantly responds to my positive thinking."

Job 22:28

Ex: "I am blessed to bless others." OR " I respond to the call for kindness in every interaction throughout my day."

I Decree...

Be Mindful

Set your mind every morning by spending the 1st 17 seconds thinking good thoughts. This will keep you in alignment with what you want because your feelings fuel your thoughts, thoughts shape your words, and your words shape your world! The moment a negative feeling arises it is accompanied by a negative thought. This spiral of negative thinking is difficult to stop once it gains momentum. Taking the first moments of waking to set your mind keeps you from placing your situation over your destination. Be sure not to make them conditional thoughts or statements like

"It's a beautiful day!" or "Thank God the sun is shining and the flowers are in bloom!". These are conditional thoughts. What if it's raining, or snowing and spring is delayed once again? Is it still a beautiful day? Are you thankful without the sun? Instead, stick with thoughts peppered with feeling like "these pillows are comfortable" "I love the way these sheets feel against my toes…" "What a great day to be alive"

Job 22:28

"I am thankful that I am alive". You can also do this before you go to bed, especially when you've had a less than stellar day!

No More Stinking Thinking!

All things, even moments that we don't prefer, are working to bring us our best life and create the best version of US! Just like you can decree the POSITIVE, you can also decree the NEGATIVE. If you say "I can't do..." "It will never..." "I'm so broke"

"This relationship is over" "No one loves me" you cannot be surprised when what you speak manifest! WATCH YOUR WORDS!

Whenever you are faced with situations or people that oppose what you envision and believe, take charge of your thinking and DECREE " All things are working for my good and my destiny. Even moments I don't prefer."

" I am thankful for the lesson in this moment and look forward to seeing how it will help me obtain my goals." This places you in control of your thought patterns.

The Decree Challenge

There are many experts on change and how long it takes to create a new habit, and I am not here to chime in on length of time it will take to create your best self. What I know is that consistency is the key to manifestation. Can you commit to speaking well of your life mentally, physically, and financially for the next 30 days? Great!

I'm glad you chose YOU!

Job 22:28

Instructions:

1. Identify 3 areas of your life to DECREE (relationships, attitude, employment, direction, opportunity, purpose, finances, weight loss, etc...).
2. Create 1-3 affirmations for each area (no more than 10 affirmations).
    a. You can also write them on sticky notes and place them on your mirror. Looking at yourself while you say them is VERY effective in changing mindset and increasing your faith.
3. DECREE your affirmations every morning (and before you go to bed if you REALLY want to see things manifest).
4. Spend 30 minutes a day meditation of the mental picture of your best self. Swim in those emotions and thank God for your journey.
5. Before you go to bed check your emotions and thoughts. If they are negative make sure you RESET by sitting in the silence of the emotions attached to what you envision.

6. DO NOT RUSH THE PROCESS! INSTEAD ENJOY THE JOURNEY! The best stories of success are created from experiences. Let your journey create a joy that can only come from wisdom gained through experiences!
7. CELEBRATE and SHARE when what you've decreed manifest! Do not be surprised if what you desire shows up before the 30 days are up.

*** Keep an open mind and look for unexpected ways to see what you decree! I affirmed that I would see love throughout my day. I was surprised when I received compliments on my looks, or random messages from old students telling me how much they loved me. THOSE WERE BOTH FORMS OF LOVE! ***

 Below you will find some shortcut affirmations in case you get stuck and don't know what to say.

Job 22:28

Financial Decrees:

The wisdom to obtain wealth is mine and I am open to multiple streams of income.

I am abundance and overflow

I Decree financial stability

Mindset Decree:
I believe success is possible
All things are working for my highest good
I AM the physical manifestation of the I AM in the earth and ANYTHING IS POSSIBLE.

Relationship Decree:
I am unconditionally loved, honored, and cherished.
My relationships are mutually beneficial, productive, and synergistic.
I am supported and people speak well of me whenever my name is mentioned.
Decree for Self Esteem:
I am beautiful
This body possesses all that it needed to be successful.

I am fearfully and wonderfully made.
I have a commanding charismatic presence.
I am a magnet for success!

Decree Hodgepodge:

I am legacy
I am a world changer
I am connected to the source and all is mine
I agree with the plans for my life.
I am a millionaire
I am healthy, wealthy, and whole
I am forgiveness
I am kindness
I am a consistent flow of creativity

Lastly, HAVE FUN! Make a Decree Playlist to amp up the excitement! Scream it at the top of your lungs; smile while you command your day!

Remember: *How* you say is just as important as *what* you

Job 22:28

Day 1

Make Your Decree

A Moment of Joy in My Day

_____
_____
_____
_____
_____
_____
_____

Did you observe any interesting interactions? Did you experience unexpected positive conversations? Where there any moments of contrast, and did you reset before bed? What was your emotional state today?

Become the change you want to see in the world!

Job 22:28

Day 2

A Moment of Clarity in My Day

When you realize your prosperity is connected to positivity, you will refuse to waste your time being preoccupied with negativity.

A mindset is a terrible thing to waste! Set your mind on positive and productive before you leave the house. Decide what day YOU want to have and make it great!

Job 22:28

Day 3

A Moment of Opportunity in My Day

Enjoy each day as if it were specifically designed for you to: succeed, make mistakes, grow, learn, encourage others, be uplifted, produce, enlighten, be kind, and beautiful.

Make Your Decree

"Whoever wants to embrace life and see the day fill up with good, Here's what you do: **Say nothing evil or hurtful" 1 Peter 3:10**

Job 22:28

Day 4

___

A Teachable Moment in My Day

___

Did you observe any interesting interactions? Did you experience unexpected positive conversations? Where there any moments of contrast, and did you reset before bed? What was your emotional state today?

Make Your Decree

The only competitor you should be concerned with is the one in the mirror.

Job 22:28

Day 5

___

A Moment of Great Expectation in My Day

___

Successful people understand that they must stand in great expectation even if no one else sees what's just beyond the horizon.

Make Your Decree

What goes into someone's mouth does not defile them, but what comes out of their mouth, that is what Defiles them. Matthew 15:11

Job 22:28

Day 6

___

A Moment of Love in My Day

___

The universe obeys the voice of the one person who dares to play happiness on repeat. Successful people know it is a choice and privilege to acknowledge how fortunately blessed they are.

Make Your Decree

I am a giver of life.
I am a world changer.
I am Legacy.

Job 22:28

Day 7

_____
_____
_____
_____
_____
_____
_____
_____
_____
_____
_____
_____
_____
_____
_____
_____
_____
_____
_____
_____

A Moment of Happiness in My Day

_____
_____
_____
_____
_____

Did you observe any interesting interactions? Did you experience unexpected positive conversations? Where there any moments of contrast, and did you reset before bed? What was your emotional state today?

Make Your Decree

Decree from your Destination and not your current situation!

Job 22:28

Day 8

___

A Moment of Purpose in My Day

___

Train your mind to believe what hasn't manifested. Train your eyes to see what isn't there; and train your mouth to speak to the universe in a manner that commands respect and success.

Make Your Decree

**Post a guard at my mouth, God, set a watch at the door of my lips.
Psalm 141:3**

Job 22:28

Day 9

A Moment of Selflessness in My Day

Did you observe any interesting interactions? Did you experience unexpected positive conversations? Where there any moments of contrast, and did you reset before bed? What was your emotional state today?

Make Your Decree

Visionaries create their realities from the future of what they believe and not what they see..

Job 22:28

Day 10

A Moment of Courage in My Day

The difference between success and failure is that those who are successful get back up after they have fallen.

Make Your Decree

Whatever things are true, whatever things are noble, whatever things are just, whatever things are pure, whatever things are lovely, whatever things are of good report, if there is any virtue and if there is anything praiseworthy - meditate on these things.

Phil 4:8

Job 22:28

Day 11

A Moment of Faith in My Day

Do not judge your progress by comparing your process to others! Know that all things work together for your good, your story, and your niche!

Make Your Decree

Life is but an instrument; the key in which you play is your choice. Play in the major and not minor keys!

Job 22:28

Day 12

_____
_____
_____
_____
_____
_____
_____
_____
_____
_____
_____
_____
_____
_____
_____
_____
_____
_____

A Moment of Mercy in My Day

_____
_____
_____
_____
_____

Did you observe any interesting interactions? Did you experience unexpected positive conversations? Where there any moments of contrast, and did you reset before bed? What was your emotional state today?

Make Your Decree

Words Kill, Words Give Life... they are either poison or fruit-you choose.
Proverbs 18:21

Job 22:28

Day 13

_____
_____
_____
_____
_____
_____
_____
_____
_____
_____
_____
_____
_____
_____
_____

A Moment of Bravery in My Day

_____
_____
_____
_____
_____

A successful person has "I can do it!" on repeat on their mental playlist!

Make Your Decree

Successful people have enough wisdom to utilize the vast resources around them. There are people waiting to assist in your success who don't look like the usual suspects.

Job 22:28

Day 14

A Moment of Confidence in My Day

What's the point in having arms if you don't reach for the sky?

Make Your Decree

Let the weak say, I am strong
Joel 3:10

Job 22:28

Day 15

A Moment of Empathy in My Day

Did you observe any interesting interactions? Did you experience unexpected positive conversations? Where there any moments of contrast, and did you reset before bed? What was your emotional state today?

Make Your Decree

Reliving the negative things in life is like losing your place in a 400-page book; it always takes longer to catch up to the present and enjoy the next phase. Successful people just let it go!

Job 22:28

Day 16

A Moment of Strength in My Day

Did you observe any interesting interactions? Did you experience unexpected positive conversations? Where there any moments of contrast, and did you reset before bed? What was your emotional state today?

Make Your Decree

If an ant can carry 5000x its weight and withstand the pressure, what then are you able to carry? Face it; the opposition has no idea what you're made of!

Job 22:28

Day 17

___

A Moment of Nostalgia in My Day

___

Did you observe any interesting interactions? Did you experience unexpected positive conversations? Where there any moments of contrast, and did you reset before bed? What was your emotional state today?

Make Your Decree

...Whoever speaks to this mountain, 'Be taken up and thrown into the sea,' and does not doubt in his heart, but believes that what he says will come to pass, it will be done for him. - Mark 11:23

Job 22:28

Day 18

A Moment of Laughter in My Day

Did you observe any interesting interactions? Did you experience unexpected positive conversations? Where there any moments of contrast, and did you reset before bed? What was your emotional state today?

Make Your Decree

We must be so sure of our destination that won't be distracted by sightseeing detours.

Job 22:28

Day 19

_____
_____
_____
_____
_____
_____
_____
_____
_____
_____
_____
_____
_____
_____
_____
_____
_____

Today I Invested in Someone Else By...

_____
_____
_____
_____

Did you observe any interesting interactions? Did you experience unexpected positive conversations? Where there any moments of contrast, and did you reset before bed? What was your emotional state today?

Just say the word from where you are, and my servant will be healed.

Matthew 8:8

Job 22:28

Day 20

___

A Moment of Creativity in My Day

___

Did you observe any interesting interactions? Did you experience unexpected positive conversations? Where there any moments of contrast, and did you reset before bed? What was your emotional state today?

Make Your Decree

Successful people have enough wisdom to utilize the vast resources around them. There are people waiting to assist in your success but they don't look like the usual suspects.

Job 22:28

Day 21

_____

A Moment of Growth in My Day

_____

Did you observe any interesting interactions? Did you experience unexpected positive conversations? Where there any moments of contrast, and did you reset before bed? What was your emotional state today?

Make Your Decree

A mindset is a terrible thing to waste! Set your mind on positive and productive before you leave the house; decide what day YOU want to have and make it great.

Job 22:28

Day 22

___

A Moment of Awareness in My Day

___

Did you observe any interesting interactions? Did you experience unexpected positive conversations? Where there any moments of contrast, and did you reset before bed? What was your emotional state today?

Make Your Decree

> "... And God said, "Let there be light," and there was light."
> Genesis 1:1

Job 22:28

Day 23

___

A Moment of Thankfulness in My Day

___

Did you observe any interesting interactions? Did you experience unexpected positive conversations? Where there any moments of contrast, and did you reset before bed? What was your emotional state today?

Make Your Decree

Visionaries create their realities from the future of what they believe and not what they see!

Job 22:28

Day 24

___

A Moment of Success in My Day

___

Did you observe any interesting interactions? Did you experience unexpected positive conversations? Where there any moments of contrast, and did you reset before bed? What was your emotional state today?

Make Your Decree

Life is but an instrument; the key in which you play is your choice. Play in the major and not minor keys!

Job 22:28

Day 25

A Moment of Grace in My Day

Did you observe any interesting interactions? Did you experience unexpected positive conversations? Where there any moments of contrast, and did you reset before bed? What was your emotional state today?

Make Your Decree

Turn your list of possibilities into a book of reality.

Job 22:28

Day 26

___

A Moment of Encouragement in My Day

___

Did you observe any interesting interactions? Did you experience unexpected positive conversations? Where there any moments of contrast, and did you reset before bed? What was your emotional state today?

Make Your Decree

**...Our speech we can ruin the world, turn harmony to chaos, throw mud on a reputation, send the whole world up in smoke and go up in smoke with it...
James 3:6**

Job 22:28

Day 27

_____

A Moment of Self-Care in My Day

_____

Did you observe any interesting interactions? Did you experience unexpected positive conversations? Where there any moments of contrast, and did you reset before bed? What was your emotional state today?

Make Your Decree

If you're going to finish the course with joy, guard your torch. Don't let your fire go out, maintain your passion!

Job 22:28

Day 28

A Moment of Freedom in My Day

Did you observe any interesting interactions? Did you experience unexpected positive conversations? Where there any moments of contrast, and did you reset before bed? What was your emotional state today?

Make Your Decree

There are more possible iterations in a game of chess than there are atoms in the universe. Stop narrowing our choices and embrace the possibilities.

Job 22:28

Day 29

_____
_____
_____
_____
_____
_____
_____
_____
_____
_____
_____
_____
_____
_____
_____
_____
_____
_____
_____

A Moment of Forgiveness in My Day

_____
_____
_____
_____

Did you observe any interesting interactions? Did you experience unexpected positive conversations? Where there any moments of contrast, and did you reset before bed? What was your emotional state today?

Make Your Decree

A successful person does not respond to the negative bricks thrown at them; instead they use those bricks to build a solid foundation for their greatness

Job 22:28

Day 30

_____
_____
_____
_____
_____
_____
_____
_____
_____
_____
_____
_____
_____
_____
_____
_____

A Celebration of Pride and My Commitment to My Best Self

_____
_____
_____
_____
_____

Did you observe any interesting interactions? Did you experience unexpected positive conversations? Where there any moments of contrast, and did you reset before bed? What was your emotional state today?

Make Your Decree

Job 22:28

Make Your Decree

Job 22:28

Make Your Decree

Job 22:28

Make Your Decree

Job 22:28

Make Your Decree

Job 22:28

Make Your Decree

Job 22:28

Make Your Decree

Job 22:28

Make Your Decree

Job 22:28

Make Your Decree

Job 22:28

Make Your Decree

Job 22:28

Make Your Decree

Job 22:28

Make Your Decree

Job 22:28

Make Your Decree

Job 22:28

Make Your Decree

Job 22:28

i was created to be
EXTRAORDINARY

www.ingramcontent.com/pod-product-compliance
Lightning Source LLC
Chambersburg PA
CBHW041626220426
43663CB00001B/24